Poems by Juliet
A heart to heart discourse

Written by Juliet Kokaram Hosein

Illustrations curated by
Liann Horrel Pariag

Table of Contents

ACKNOWLEDGEMENTS

All power, honour, and glory belong to the Father, the Son, and the Holy Spirit.

I am deeply grateful to the Holy Spirit for inspiring me to write these poems, which reflect my faith and the journey of my soul.

A heartfelt thanks to my God-sent angel, Mrs. Liann Horrel Pariag (Lawyer/Author), for her unwavering encouragement, kindness, and invaluable support in making this book a reality.

I am blessed to be sixty-six years old. I was married to my beloved husband, Shaffick Hosein, now departed. Together, we raised two wonderful sons, Javid and Jeron, who are my pride and joy.

As a widow and a retiree, my life is firmly anchored in the Word of God. The scripture, *"For in Him we live and move and have our being"* (Acts 17:28), resonates deeply with me, as without Him, I am nothing.

This book is a testament to His grace and faithfulness. Thank you, Jesus, for Your boundless love and guidance.

I would like to thank every reader for choosing this Book of Poems. May God bless you.

Love and Blessings,

Juliet Kokaram Hosein

WITHOUT FURTHER ADO –
(HIS APPEARANCE IS DUE!)

Wars and more wars, rumours of wars
Pestilence and earthquakes in various places
Nations and kingdoms against each other
False prophets in all forms of fashion to smother

Time awaits no one as the days are shortened
Hey! The asteroid's already cast down from heaven;
Do you really want to experience the wrath?
For soon the rapture will occur – like that!
And you will be left behind to stir
A nightmare in tribulation's rapt...

Come on people, get real and subside –
JESUS CHRIST died on the **CROSS** for you and I
Don't you know that every knee shall bow?
Yes!.. Everyone will confess that **Jesus Christ is Lord**
'Cause He's the **ONLY SAVIOUR** and son of the creator;

So why delay for the late outcry?
Awake now! Receive Him – don't deny
And although your sins may be as crimson with ego
By reason – He'll make you clean to season

Please don't hesitate and lose your souls for amends
He wants to give you... eternal life... - my friends.

A JOURNEY TO HEARTBURN LANE

Innocently I encountered an unaided thoroughfare
With the tarnish environs of delude
As I prologue down to Heartburn Lane
Broken with a twinge of rebuke;
I questioned such a difficult path
Without knowledge and wisdom to allure
And deception of faithfulness to adhere
A misconception of flesh of one flesh
That worth a reflection to amiss…

In contemplation a small voice within
Never look back to regret an impact
But stride towards the better path
Of no hurdles and stumbling stones to hinder
As I encountered the crossroad on shore
In question of my return
No hurts anymore from now on assured
My forward march to the positive side
In peace and love my desires realize
By the straight and narrow road to secure.

A NEW LOVE IN MY LIFE

I've found a new love in my life today
After heartaches and pains of yesterday
And my life was practically dismayed and delayed
With a sad countenance to exterminate-

Supernaturally, someone knocked at my door
He graciously beckoned to come inside
As we reasoned together, He erased my sins to abide
Then gave me abundant life to reside

He's become my joy unspeakable, to glory receivable
My best friend who's closer than my mother
My adviser, my hope and spring to desire
For without Him I'm nothing – just clay in attire

He's so patient and kind to all my requests,
My Redeemer and Healer, my best to attest
The Prince of Peace and comfort to all
Truly, my Shepherd, my strength and happiness to recall

I'm so in love with Him – words just cannot say
With purity, holiness and endurance I engage
For the promised mansion awaits the marriage
To Him I acclaim more than a conqueror as my heritage.

A TRIBUTE TO MUMMY

Laundry and dirt – mummy unhurt
Cooking, washing and ironing never differ
Patience and virtue – all true
Gracious to be born from you.

Stressed and pressed yet nobly zest
Toils with joy so humbly dressed
Yet always ready for the best
Especially when I do tests.

Simple and firm to approach my world
Homework and chores you adore
Family worship at night to score
Love and respect to all encore.

Wisdom and trust our daddy's praise
Blessed and highly favoured – others amaze
Humility and prayers, your priority's concern
"Hats off to you mummy!" We salute you today.

HAPPY'S MOTHERS DAY

A TRIBUTE TO OUR MOTHER
(Dedicated to Mrs. Merle Kokaram)
Went to be with the Lord 06/04/08

A fatherless child she was
Yet nurtured and moulded with the fear of God,
An innocent wife she claimed
With heartbreak of suffering and pain
From a broken marriage she came
Not for herself but in obedience to God
To sacrifice her soul to care for not your own
And her toil was in total success!

'Cause she brought sunshine on rain
With unconditional love to zest
The rebirth of a scholar's bequest;
Hey! Her travail was not in vain –
Her efforts were worth more than rubies and pearls
As she birthed seven diamonds of joy
A heart of gold is what she maintained
'Cause she never looked back for any rewards,
She was called Blessed but now highly famed
A daughter of New Jerusalem is promptly her name –
A widow indeed, intercessor and prayer warrior,
A woman of beauty and grace
And because she feared the Lord – our queen
Henceforth she'll always be praised!

MAY GOD BLESS HER PRECIOUS SOUL.
See you in heaven Mamma!

A GENUINE MOTHER'S LOVE

You cannot be compared with worldly gifts
'Cause you birthed us into being
A chosen icon for this matchless bequest
Written on the palm of God's hand
And when that infallible change began
You took up the mantle to shine
Nurturing us from conception to birth
With unconditional love to align;

Yes – Mother!
You're more valuable than precious stones
Fine rubies, chosen silver and refined gold
Earthly materials simply cannot replace
Your golden crown of favoured grace
Enfolded with beauty from within
Furnished with endurance to maintain
Yes! Your flame never goes dim;

And even though you're in heaven or earth
Forever we are your babies alert
Therefore we honour you
With gratitude of this first-fruit gift of love
Which is incomparable to husband or wife
But a genuine mother's love to survive.

HAPPY WEDDING ANNIVERSARY

Ever since you've tied the knot
Of marriage with your vows,
You've proved to all – with faithfulness
Of being TRULY in love!

Yes! The angels rejoice
With your excellence in all accomplishments
At home, at work, and ventures everywhere…
Hey! It's a milestone of blissful years of marriage
With never a moment of lust to stray!

A compatible couple with no regrets
Showered with abundant blessings aloft –
Of peculiar priceless treasures
From a holy matrimony of course
Now precious extended families with grandchildren
To captivate your unconditional love;

An admirable couple indeed!
And with the fear of God and Christ as your head
The reward for your marriage's assured.

A TRIBUTE TO DAD - OUR HERO

As a good and faithful father
Your purpose on this earth was fulfilled
By your excellent gift of giving and caring
And your outstanding character of being a workaholic
Even though your health was threatened
Your love for us never hardened
You continued to pursue with enthusiasm until the end
Yes Dad! We salute you

'Cause in your teens, you encountered the role of a man
As you bravely ventured into the field of work
To provide for your loved ones with esteem on demand
A caring son and brother was your title from birth,
So much more you deserved to fulfil your career
Yet because of your supremacy in workmanship
And your ambition and determination
You kept accomplishing everything perfect for us

Hey – Although sometimes you demise
Yet your perseverance to endeavours never decline
Thus impacting the character of the envision father
And with His fear and your choice in JESUS
Your soul is secured in Him and with His assurance
Of a mansion in Heaven,
Your soul will rest in peace eternally.

BE NOT DECEIVED – GOD IS NOT MOCKED

So you think you are Mr. Big Stuff?
Always believing a lie for the truth
And expounding evil for good in God's sight;
You flatter yourself to be called macho
With the image of a beast from the East....

You live in closed doors like a loony from hell –
Not only an abuser, adulterer and tormentor
But a false accuser, lunatic and hypocrite
Soon you will reap your harvest!
You plant seeds of corruption in your flesh
Yet you want health and prosperity in excess –

You despise God but demand His consecrate
With no regress of being a tormentor and persecutor;
You're truly a vessel of dishonour and debate
Because you hate instruction and correction
Your determination makes you a horrid dictator –
Awake now! You hard-hearted, stiff-necked infidel

When God chastises – you scoff Him instead
Why? You've become a reprobate and apostate –
So please be admonished wise fool of anguish
For the wrath of God will soon inflate
Just repent today for tomorrow is too late
And you'll surely receive your own merit...

"Be not deceived – God is not mocked".

BEWARE – THE ADVERSARY

Sweet words as smooth as honey and oil
Forced smiles with love of guile and turmoil
An effort that's worth enough for the catch
Yet stabs at the back with arrows to attack…

A determined attitude to get your ego
With kisses of betrayal to your face in macho
A personality of schizophrenia invade
An attribute to heal your wounds in charade;

A peculiar character of cupid profuse
And an innocent being is deceived to parade –
As a fool is fallen in the trap of lions
With a narrow escape of return to irony;

A regret to survive the journey's align
With bitterness and sorrows to mature by time –
A fragile heart is wounded and bruised
Which can never be exhibited for excuse

But who's to be blamed at the end of it all?
The cunning fox just smiles with his jaw
Like the cat's meal of canary to digest
An accomplished mission of the enemy's success.

BEWARE – (THE STRANGE WOMAN)

My sons – my sons I admonish you today
Awake and be conscious that your minds do not drift
For the spirit of Jezebel is roaming to demand
Your precious life to hellfire with her magic wand…

The Commandments of God are right – you must know
Abstain from the evil woman tonight – yes, the whore!
For the flattery of her tongue will weaken you to melt
And lust after her outward beauty with guilt to your health;

Don't you know if you go over the edge you will fall?
For the man who lives by the sword will die by this call
Also, he who lusts after his neighbour's wife
Shall not be innocent in the day of judgement…

Yes! Whoever commits adultery is a fool
As he lacks understanding and wisdom like a mule,
He simply destroys his own soul to become
A victim of dishonour with his name on a scroll;

So listen carefully – register these words of advice
And let not your heart decline to regrets in life
Thus keep God's Commandments and receive
His Righteousness and Salvation – The Everlasting Gift.

INDISCIPLINED CHILDREN IN SCHOOLS

Children, children! Hear my genuine cry
Big clan, small clan be humbly advised
A good character is far better than refined gold
It cannot be either bought or sold;

Why are you so callously minded?
When in fact you should be moulded and guided
With high self-esteem and control
To accomplish the dreams and aspirations of your role,

Yet without thought and counsel from Sir
You venture into strife and resentment to stir
Instead of rebuke and correction incur
You reject diligence to excel in your career
And succumb to war and despair!

Too late – too late shall be the outcry
If not admonished and be reconciled
Awake now! You're the future of the world
So receive your chastisement with dignity and pride-

A wise man follows instruction- don't you know?
A gracious woman retains her honour
One who seeks goodness shall receive favour
And only he who loves knowledge is wise.

MAN SHALL NOT LIVE BY BREAD ALONE
(Dedicated to my earthly Father Albert Kokaram)

I remember exceptional times of old to unfold
No luxury – only fantasies to withhold
Sometimes no meat to taste – only bread on our plate
Yet there was love to comfort and strengthen us dictate

As we endeavoured towards improvement to gain
Only His grace was sufficient for us to obtain
Surely – we depended on Him to sustain
As our earthly father worked hard to maintain

Conscientiously, he taught us wisdom to love
Although being a fatherless son of the soil – he constrained
Jesus – his only hope and trust to depend
As he fervently prayed and read The Bible anon

Because of his effectual, righteous prayers for his children's children
It's a blessing to rejoice and announce
The achievements of all his grandchildren in the sun
With scholastic doctorate and merits on the run

It is written "Man shall not live by bread alone"
This man acknowledged God as his very own
He bruised his knees at night for us while others slept
In result to total attainment of bliss and success.

PRESENT CHOICES – FUTURE DESTINY

My sons - my sons! Be cautious and learn
To listen to your mother whose daily prayers yearn
For The Fear of God to saturate your brains
With knowledge, wisdom to understanding
The kingdom of God to reign

Yes! This precious gift is not in vain
Ask and you will be given to maintain
The pleasures of Him in everything ascertain
For life is overshadowed with experiences to unfold-
So be admonished and become the head not the tail

A leader and not a follower – instead-
An inspiration and perfect role model in your careers
So prioritize life – Don't compromise -
For success and prosperity, peace and love will archive
Hence with Shakespeare's vision of "All's well that ends well"

Will sanction your present choices to determine
Your future's destiny in approval to your eternity.

SARAH – THE COVERNANTED ONE
(Dedicated to my grandmother – A genuine Widow Indeed)

Sarah, Fairdosa Maude Lois – Kokaram my dame
A distinctive lady of beauty and character became
Young you met Andrew- your knight in shining amour
As you attested your love and marriage with God to honour

Lovingly you birthed three jewels of joy
Sadly you became a young widow as fate befall-
Still you toiled tirelessly to uphold your inheritance
With dignity and love you became a mother of all

Granny! As you were so graciously called
The virtuous one who excelled them all
Filled with Wisdom, courage and strength indeed
Singing praise and praying psalms to rejoice

Oh! How I wish you were here once again
To gift me those treasured rag dolls and rugs that you blend
And those awesome plants, fruits and flowers to décor
Serenaded at nights with songs and true stories of old in adore

A lover of nature and faithfulness to God
A woman of discretion, chaste obedience and love
Truly you were the chosen role model on earth to portray
Beyond a shadow of a doubt you're safe in paradise today.

32

Sometimes

SOMETIMES

Sometimes I wish I were a cricket cap
To live on Brian Lara's head
But that wouldn't do any good
Yes! He'll throw me off when he goes to bed

Sometimes I wish I were a shining star
To give the whole world light
Nah - that wouldn't do any good either
Because I'll only live at nights,

Sometimes I wish I were a sun roof hood
Of a brand new Tesla motor car
But I guess that wouldn't serve any purpose
I'll get soaked in when it rains

But hey! I'm glad I'm not a cricket cap
A shining star nor the sun-roof hood of a Tesla motorcar
But I'm proud to be the child of the Most High God
To be the head and not the tail
The above and not below
The leader and not the follower
With wisdom, integrity and understanding
And most importantly – The fear of God
To guide and direct me into all truth
And I'm proud to be exactly who I am.

A TRIBUTE TO FATHER

Beloved fathers
Don't you know that your title is sovereign?
When God ordained you to become dad
And blessed you with the gift of mom to regard
To love and appreciate till death do you part
You became HIS representative on earth to impart:

The mantle of authority in your home to provide
The important role He predestined you to mould
He knew that you would never substantiate
A pebble for bread in the plate
Instead His priesthood embedded you to appreciate
Impacting the matchless character of this envision role

With good prophetic words on your children to uphold

Yes Father - If you only know who you really are -
A chosen son of The Most High God!
And with His unconditional love…. Indeed! You're requested to bless and not curse
And govern the home with headship and love
By guidance and tuition from the manual above

Hence embedding the Fear of God in the heart
And guarding that Arc that it would never depart.

THE MARRIAGE

When they fell in love with each other -
Their hearts desired to be together
Perpetually they didn't want to be separated
So they ventured into marriage;

Instantly as they sanctioned the vows with God
Miraculously his rib was placed into hers
The same flesh and bones of one body covenanted
Love blossomed then but soon disappeared unknown-

She kept the promise of faithfulness
But his spirit of lust overtook his mind to decay,
He betrayed her so relentlessly without remorse
But she pursued with patience and endurance of course

To gain his trust and love in assurance;
She gave him her youth and innocence with dignity
But he took it for granted so insensitively
She gave love and respect unconditionally

Yet he contemplated unfaithfulness disrespectfully;
True love is being sorry when at flaw
Never to look back with layouts to implore
But simply forgive and forget being unequally yoked

And strive towards a better life with God's gift of love to overflow.

THE RESURRECTION

Wake up! Wake up - It's resurrection morn
The stone has rolled away anon
Jesus Christ - The ONLY Saviour conquered the grave
As He defeated the devil from hell to brave;
YES! Now ascended in heaven's reign
As Lord and King that cannot feign
Alas! The Holy Spirit now descends
To direct and guide in everything to amend;

Wake up - shout out! It's resurrection morn
The fulfilment of scriptures now realized -
The promise of Almighty God verified,
Behold! EMMANUEL - our God's in us
And the keys of heaven He gave –
Without a shadow of a doubt
The Resurrection power to bind and loose on earth
By His matchless name JESUS from birth;

Wake up – Arise! It's resurrection morn!
Aloft! Now possess His risen crown
To trample over snakes and horns
In accomplishment to carry on
Yes! The authority to do all things through Christ
The resurrection and life to survive
Whose innocent Blood was officially shed
In redemption for mortals to overcome ahead.

HAPPY EASTER!

THE REVELATION OF CHRISTMAS
God's perfect gift to mankind

Because of God's unconditional love for mankind
He sent His only Begotten son –
"The Great I am"
Yes! THE SAVIOUR was born to give man a second chance
Thus the perfect gift of love was portrayed with no resistance….

On that holy night love transcended…
As the herald angels descended
Joy bells triumph as the King was manifested in the humblest birth
For He left His most majestic throne of supremacy
To be born of a favoured virgin in a manger,
"A light to lighten the Gentiles and the glory of the people of Israel"
For unto us was born on that Holy Christmas morn - Emmanuel
Upon the throne of David the son of God was given
His name is Wonderful, Counsellor, Mighty God
The Everlasting Father and Prince of Peace;

His promised restoration of divine government accomplished;
So let us celebrate this Yuletide season in appreciation
To share His word in deeds and thoughts with participation
To everyone throughout the world
As we glorify the birthday of
This matchless Christ-child –
JESUS CHRIST – THE ONLY SAVIOR OF THE WORLD
Who came to establish order with judgment and justice forever.

THE TRUE MEANING OF CHRISTMAS
The First Noel

It was on that momentous starry – silent, holy night
When God's Perfect gift of Love was demonstrated–
As the King of Kings was born in the humblest birth
Yes! God incarnate was manifested in a manger at Bethlehem
The Holy sinless man child of the chosen Virgin Mary
And The Only Saviour of the world – THE MESSIAH
Was born to save mankind from his sins to Eternity;
Gloria in Excelsis Deo! The herald angels rejoiced
As The matchless Christ child transcended from heaven
"Immanuel" God with us is celebrated in Nativity by Divinity.

Shalom Aleichem! Peace be unto you as it's written
"For unto us is born, unto us a Son is given and the government shall
be upon His shoulder and His name is Wonderful, Counsellor, The
Mighty God, The Everlasting Father, The Prince of Peace" The
Great I am - The Son of the Highest
Who shall reign over Israel forever and of His Kingdom shall be no
end -
"A light to lighten the Gentiles and the glory of thy people Israel"
Halleluiah! The Word was made flesh of The Trinity!

The Alpha and Omega- The beginning and the end,
The Lily of the Valley- The Bright and Morning Star,
The Eternal Light- The Son of Righteousness,
The bread of Life and the Living Water
Was born to die for our sins on Calvary's Cross
To redeem us from the curse of the Law into Victory.

So as we celebrate this precious, blessed Christmas season
With gift exchanges to friends and loved ones everywhere…
Let's share God's perfect gift of Jesus with Salvation and
Reconciliation to all with peace and goodwill throughout the year.

(Merry Christmas everyone)

UNCOMPARABLE

You cannot be compared with worldly gifts
Your life is most important to us
God gave us you to appreciate and cherish
Because He loves you so much
Words cannot say how much we love you
'Cause you're a good husband and father,
You've always been there for us
Always providing materials' best
Making us comfortable at home and at play
Truly you've worked hard to accomplish everything,
So what can I give you, I guess
All that I have belong to you under God
But there's something more than gold in my soul
All my love, prayers, and faithfulness
Most importantly Christ who lives within
The most precious gift from God to mankind
So I humbly present Him to you my love.

UNIVERSAL CHILDREN'S DAY

Even though I may be a fatherless child
Or from a broken single-parent home instead -
Yet I have every right to be unconditionally loved
By my parents and kin especially now

Hey! I cannot be compared to worldly gems
I'm predestined with purpose to blend
Hence my reason to obey and fear God
Which gives me the right to survive my sod,

Therefore my right to be given food and housed
Most importantly encouraged by those I love
And respected for my ideas and crafts
As I continue in meekness from above,

I need to be educated and well learned
By both teachers and parents who are concerned
Also to enjoy playing with my toys
With no compromising of being foiled;

And even though I may be sad or glad
Yet I have every right to be secured by guard
For one cannot enter God's kingdom unless
He becomes an innocent child like me to assess.

WHAT A MAN SOWS - THAT WILL HE REAP

Hey! You want to sow corn seeds and reap peas instead
Where did you get that philosophy in your head?
Don't you know The Word of God is TRUTH
What is man sows- that is exactly what he will reap

Hence I admonish you carefully, be wise and subside
Forget all your foolish ideologies and pride
If you sow the seeds of corruption in your flesh
You'll receive damnation of eternity in hell to remorse

Truly! You can't expect to sow hatred and reap love
Nor can you sow wickedness and reap goodness from above
Please don't be deluded by illusions of confusion;
When you sow deceit you'll reap complexity

No doubt about it- God's Word is unaltered
Now- If you want peace, love and happiness to follow
With good health, prosperity and good success tomorrow
Sow good seeds of God's command and you'll reap

The benefits of goodness and mercies throughout eternity.

WHEN THE GOING GETS TOUGH

When my victory is about to manifest itself,
The enemy just roars like a lion instead,
And predisposes akin to a tidal wave
To flood my vision with doubts and disgrace,
Seeking to devour my authority to inflate,
But cannot comprehend my standard to dictate.

So I quickly succumb to prayer and meditate
To overcome these stumbling blocks in faith,
And whenever I try to be nice I realize
The hurdles just rise to tempt my strive,
With anger to resort and compromise,
In questions that seem aggressive to faith.

Yet with prayer and supplications not to deviate,
Hence petition my requests to Him who arbitrate,
With eyes to and fro from the earth to the sky,
Watching every move I formulate to alibi,
Yet in stumbles and falls, He embraces my calls.

For whenever I cry - Abba, my Lord - He reminds,
In reflection of His immutable word:
"When the enemy comes in like a flood,
The Spirit of the Lord will lift up a standard against him."

ECSTASY

Have you ever been to the clouds alone
To experience sweet peace that cannot be atoned?

So when life gets rough with sensitivity ruined
I quickly sojourn to His ambiance aloft
Where no one else except the Lord
Will converse in thoughts aloud

A precious flash of peace unfold
Is what I yearn my heart to hold,

So when the floods overflow
With unchanged environs all around
Incomprehensive with the flesh of conflict
Which draws me closer to the Father's drift

I enthusiastically resort to Him in love
To surrender all sophisticated attributes of doubt
And reach His globe in the clouds on high
Enwrapped with diamonds in the sky

Where there's joy unspeakable and peace understandable;
Overwhelmed with love that become my Ecstasy.
Behold! Reality thump with the unbelievable embrace
Of a supernatural intervention of the Holy Ghost experience.

JAVID

My dearly beloved first-born son - Javid, Grayham
A tribute to you this 21st Birthday

As I remember the days of yesterday -
When you were just an outstanding baby playing with toys
Awaiting the moments to become mature
With visions and actions to adore

Yet redeeming your time with JESUS assure;

Lo! Before the reality of ages be gone
From kindergarten and High School to UWI anon -
Your charming personality of humility and kindness
Endorsed with high morals continue to reign

With dedication and motivation by obedience to maintain
In perseverance towards excellence to retain;

Yes! - My adored son - Your inception in our lives
Would always be treasured with unmerited blessings
That cannot be measured

Now officially an adult to apprehend - be admonished
Always exemplify your life with Christ to realize your vision
And accomplish your rewards to gratify your mission
To sanction the perfect role model to destine.

We love you!

HAPPY 21ST BIRTHDAY

JERON

Just the other day you were birthed by plan
As the angels rejoiced in the Hosein's clan
A little prince to cherish and care...
Hurray! The priceless baby boy is here to adhere

With enthusiasm as mummy Juliet molded you dear
By positive confessions to nurture ahead -
And God's immeasurable blessings
To saturate your being alas!

An honourable, tall, handsome young man matured
A predestined image is manifested to become
And as you braved your way with God's fear
With a passion to excel and accomplish your goal;

A good role model for this generation to surround...
A fanatic of sports of all sorts to resound
And bachelor's degree accomplished so divine
With a passion for décor and perfection to admire

By distinguished taste to galore in good success
However, through it all my son -you've only just begun
As I await to see your Godly equally - yoked bride
With a brighter and prosperous future ahead.

A TRIBUTE TO MOTHER

We pay tribute to you dearly beloved mothers
On this special Mothers' Day
Because God has given you this gift
To birth us without any delay-
He predesignated us and formed us in your womb
And set you apart with the best heart
To love and cherish even though we may be apart;

How can we say thank you Mom!
For everything you've done for us?
Words cannot utter how much we appreciate
Your input in our lives as we meditate,
Your genuine love simply cannot compare
To rubies and pearls and gold everywhere
Your strength and courage with amazing grace
To oversee our lives to fill this place
And your pride and joy in everything you do
Especially taking care of us all anew...

So without further - ado - We honour you
With a crown of immeasurable gratitude
And unconditional love
Yes! You are simply incomparable to anyone else.

HAPPY EASTER

It's more than two thousand years ago
When JESUS CHRIST – The only begotten Son of God
Went on Calvary's Cross to die for mankind
He was despised and rejected of His own
A man of sorrows and acquainted with grief
And we did hide our faces from Him as the scripture declares
"He was despised and we esteemed Him not.
But He was wounded for our transgressions,
He was bruised for our iniquities,
The chastisement of our peace was upon Him,
And with His stripes we are healed."

So by His Unfailing and Redeeming LOVE- We remember
His most humiliating death on the Cross – GOOD FRIDAY
When His precious innocent blood was shed
To purchase us from the curse of the law
Which were handed down by our forefathers
Deceived by the serpent in the Garden of Eden...

Yes! Jesus being God's incarnate
Experienced death, hell, and the grave
To successfully defeat the devil in hell
And victoriously arose from the tomb on EASTER SUNDAY
Indeed! He's alive forevermore...

Hence we celebrate His death and resurrection
With VICTORY in EASTER! AMEN
Hallelujah to The Lamb of God who takes away the sins of the
world.

A THANKSGIVING BLESSING

Bless the Lord, O my soul—
Bless His Holy Name!

Who am I, and what is my name?
A child of Almighty God, adopted by Him,
To give thanks gratefully with a heart of gratitude.
For GOD so loved the world that He gave
His only begotten Son, JESUS, to die on Calvary's Cross,
So that we might have eternal life in Heaven
And become joint heirs with Him.

Yes! His mercy endures forever,
His goodness extends to all generations.
Hey! Are we His blessing? Are we His praise?
What have we done in return for His grace?

He commands us to love unreservedly and give cheerfully,
Never looking back for rewards gainfully.
And manifested blessings will unfold successfully,
With joy, peace, and prosperity incredibly.

Hey! Did we give alms and offerings today?
For the Lord is our Shepherd—we shall not lack.
Surely goodness and mercy shall follow us constantly.
His Word is Truth, and His promises are Amen.

Can we partake of His heavenly supper that is prepared?
Yes, we can, if we only believe.
The Lord—our Redeemer and everlasting strength,
The Great I Am and Ancient of Days.

Yes, indeed! It is a blessing to be a blessing.

Happy Thanksgiving, everyone!

GRANDMA

We pay tribute to you, Grandma,
For celebrating the milestone of eighty years -
A treasured gift by God himself
For highly esteeming Him and denying self,
Hence conquering obstacles of stumbling blocks
And polishing them into stepping stones;

Therefore we honour you with appreciation
For making us happy throughout the years
By anointing our heads with coconut oil
And moulding us with love and prayers,
For bathing us with carali bush
To heal our bodies from heat and rash,
For wetting our appetites with hot bake and butter
And Indian delicacies on Divali to cutter,

Also mending our clothes from torn to stitches
And miscellaneous which we took for kicks,
So as you celebrate this God-gifted day
We say "hats off" for three score and twenty
And thousands more to destiny in eternity.

HAPPY BIRTHDAY!

You cannot be compared with worldly gifts;
Your life is most important to us.
God gave us you to appreciate and cherish
Because He loves you so much.
Words cannot say how much we love you -
You're a good husband, father, brother, and son,
Always there, providing your best
To make us comfortable.

Truly you've worked hard to accomplish your goals,
So what can I give you today, my dear?
All that I have is God's abundant blessings
And something more than gold in my soul:
All my love, prayer, and faithfulness,
Most importantly Christ who lives within -
The most precious gift from God to man.

So I humbly present Him to you with love,
And as you receive Him, you'll be made perfect -
Spiritually, mentally, and physically.
May God Bless you.

HIS STRENGTH IS PERFECT IN MY WEAKNESS

When predicaments in my life derive,
I tend to retaliate and contemplate my survive.
When I'm hurt and alone in sore,
I become discontented and succumb to deplore -
Becoming mediocre and miserably insecure,
Unknowingly that my faith is assess to implore.

In audacity, I seek God in arrest
And inaudibly question my test,
Only to be told by His uncompromising word
That His grace is sufficient for me steadfastly.
But beyond my comprehension in aggression,
I forebear the agony of humiliation
And fail to realize my victory's recurrence.

Oh yes - He's done it repeatedly - supernaturally;
He reverses every fiery dart targeted to me
And turns around every evil situation to victory.
So I humbly apologize for my faithlessness and endorse:
His strength is perfect in my weakness, of course.

HAPPY THANKSGIVING

How can we say, "Thank You, Lord?"
Words cannot utter how much we appreciate
Your unconditional love—by giving us JESUS,
The Blessed Saviour of the world.
Infilling the Holy Spirit, our Comforter unfolds,
With enduring mercies, forever goodness,
And incredible grace for daily miracles.

How can we say, "Thank You, Lord?"
When You shed Your innocent blood on the cross,
To redeem us from the curse of the law,
And initiated Your LOVE on Calvary,
In demonstration by death to the core.
When You defeated Satan in hell to acclaim
Our VICTORY through Your resurrection fame.

How can we say, "Thank You, Lord?"
For the adoption to call You "Abba—Father,"
With boldness before Your throne of grace,
To lay our petitions before Your face.
For the keys of heaven, with all authority,
To bind and loose all things into eternity.

Yes, Lord! On this gifted Thanksgiving Day,
We humbly bow in appreciation,
For Your unfathomable blessings of:

Salvation, Redemption, Healing, Deliverance,
Peace, Love, Prosperity, and joy.
And most importantly, this precious breath to say:
"Thank You, Lord, for life today."

"Let everything that hath breath … Praise the Lord!"

IN EVERYTHING GIVE GOD PRAISE

Why do we often murmur and complain?
When we're troubled and going down the drain,
Maybe it's disobedience with domain—
Just like God's chosen who are blessed and sustained,
And delivered out of bondage to remain.

And although hand-picked as the apple of His eye,
With His steadfast and unconditional love to abide,
Yet we complain with no alibi,
To give Him praise from all that's within—
Only selfishness with resentment to refrain,
Giving glory and praise to the enemy in vain,
Who positioned us just not to confess,
"Thank You, Lord, for life today."

When will we learn to give God praise?
Even though situations may be dreary and dismayed,
Yet He comforts and assists in all unfeigned,
And predicaments should not govern our reign.
So, in everything we must praise His name.

A TRIBUTE TO THE CHOSEN FATHER

It is because of your loving kindness, commitment, and dedication
We recognize your unique character and with utmost respect,
We pay tribute to you on this special day,
As a well-deserved chosen earthly father.

Yes—you have toiled hard by the sweat of your brow
As you honestly ventured into the field of work
To provide for your loved ones with esteem on demand.
Yet you never gave your children a pebble for bread;
Dear Father—your title is sovereign!

'Cause you are the guard, guardian, and governor of your home,
And with your faithfulness and instruction from above,
You will be the priest, prophet, and provider as God commands.
Truly by your successful vision—your children did not perish,
Thus impacting the matchless moral fibre of the envision role,
The blessed father and head of the home.

We therefore graciously salute you as we say, "Hats off today,"
For with God's chastisement, you'll become a chosen vessel,
And with His fear—He'll prolong your years.
Yes—with your hope in righteousness—He'll flourish you with
gladness.

May God Bless You!

THE PERFECT GIFT

Take God's perfect gift of Christ and live it
Appreciate His love and freely give it.
Give the best in everything you do,
'Cause Jesus Christ was born to identify you anew.

Therefore love your neighbour as yourself—
It is the precise word of God to regard in oneself.
First, love the Lord with all your heart,
And the rest of the commandments will follow to impart.

Thus, Christ will be seen in you,
For God loves you beyond the shadow of a doubt,
That He sent His only Son, Jesus, to die on your account,
So that you might receive His everlasting gift—
Salvation with no regrets of eternity in the pit.

His salvation will become your righteousness reward,
Healing and deliverance, peace and love in one accord,
Prosperity and joy, hope and faith to uphold,
All wrapped in this Perfect Gift for you to behold.

MY NEW IDENTITY

Although I may be earthly fatherless,
Yet I received the adoption to call Him Father,
For behold what manner of love I received,
To be graciously called His daughter.

Sometimes when I'm dejected and hurt,
His comfort strengthens me to uphold,
Then my new identity in Christ is realized,
Being washed in His blood to scrutinize.

'Cause His steadfast love never cease to amaze,
He's become my daily source to adhere and appraise,
Yes—with Jesus Christ—my Lord and Saviour,
I can accomplish anything with faith and power.

Hence—I've become a peculiar person,
A chosen model to direct and sojourn,
'Cause He's never given a pebble for bread,
But every perfect gift to enjoy instead.

For He's The Great I Am—the master of all,
The King of Kings—the Lord of Lords!
I've become a joint heir with Him to gain,
Furthermore to remain with His name.

IF IT HAD NOT BEEN THE LORD WHO WAS ON MY SIDE

If it had not been the Lord who was on my side,
I would have surely been driven by the tide to deride
By virtue of betrayal without an inception for a cause,
But Jesus Christ intervened just in time at my pause.

I was too hurt to outreach at that moment of my mordancy,
As I succumbed to the flesh in peculiarity to fantasy,
But hey—although I slipped I did not totally fall—
Cause Jesus held me up with ordered feet to stand tall.

My heart was broken, I was so much deceived,
Because my forgiveness was never to be relieved,
I realized my love was taken for granted,
So I relinquished unto the other side impeded and resented.

Yes—I almost lost my sanity with all regrets for life,
Guess what?—only my prayer partners were there at my side,
To intercede on my behalf with groans before the Throne,
At the feet of the cross where their petitions were atone.

As my Savior received me in His open arms to mend,
He said He'd never forsake me—not even condemn,
But would be with me always even unto the end,
So I renewed my life in His Blood that was shed on Calvary—once
again.

Thank You Lord Jesus for this sound mind You gave,
Not only that—but power and love to forgive,
Authority to trample over demons from hell,
A beginning each day of my life to live and be well.

A VISITATION

'T was a dream I recalled—a battle of war and despair,
Accompanied by soldiers to a dungeon of deplore.
A huge metal gate was opened and I was beckoned
To proceed in a boat captained by an identity unknown;

How He paddled that boat so gracefully,
Far out in the middle of the sea to placidity.
As I beheld ecstasy that cannot be described,
I remembered precious rainbow diamonds falling from the sky;

He didn't say a word to me, nor did I see His face,
He sat in perfect stature with His long white gown in glaze.
His beauty and charisma were truly of a kind,
Yet there was something about Him—Oh yes, His Divine!

When brought back to shore, I questioned in awe,
Who was that person—Was he an angel in disguise?
And to my surprise was told to realize—
His Majesty!
JESUS CHRIST - THE KING OF KINGS!

Immediately I awoke only to recall my present calamities,
YES—My Lord visited me in assurance that He was with me
To comfort and sustain in endurance and travail.
Today I praise His name for His promised return to gain.

THE BETRAYAL

Oh! How I loved him, it was ecstasy experienced,
As we sanctioned our wedding vows to love and behold.
I really thought he'd love and cherish me in supplication,
But little did I know was a deception with affliction.

Why was I so foolish? I questioned myself in misery.
Was it a dream? I lamented to believe with antagonism.
After two months—I resolved to annul in wisdom and peace,
With the point of no return to my destiny at ease.

But no! I endured with long suffering, patience, and love,
Only to receive abuse and betrayal that abhorred,
Physically, mentally, socially, and spiritually injected undeserved,
Yet still I loyally contemplated with directions from above.

My blessings were manifested with two wonderful boys,
Whom I treasure this day with thanksgiving and rejoice.
"What God has joined together, let no man put asunder,"
I sanction in meditation of my daily calendar.

A score and more is gone but to little avail—instead,
I continue to submit to him in faithfulness ahead,
With objection and rejection in dilemma offend,
When will this storm be over?—I prayerfully agend.

Behold my Comforter whispered—"I am the witness between you,
For indeed you are the promised one with me.
I have made you one to uphold a godly seed.
Be of good courage, for vengeance is mine and I will repay."

BE YE NOT UNEQUALLY YOKED
(The story of the marriage between a lamb and a wolf)

"I'm sorry I've made a mistake," says the lamb to her father.
"You see that sheep I married was a sly wolf in disguise.
His words were soft as oil, but his thoughts were filled with war,
He said he loved me dearly but despised me to the core.

His speech is often sullen and he seldom speaks the truth,
Yet degrades me horribly only to hurt me innocently.
Boasts of his adultery with no thought of my concern,
Deals me treacherously and declares I am insane.
Frustrates me tediously, but who am I to blame?

"I'm sorry Father, please forgive me," again pleads the lamb.
"After twenty-one years of betrayal, I'm so hurt and distraught,
To become a chaste fool, having fallen for him being my first.
Yea—if only I had wings, I would have fled,
For my desire is to go to heaven instead.
Yet although my heart is sorely pained,
Still, I'll continue to call on Your name.

JEHOVAH—the most High over all the earth,
'Cause You've never left me, even before my birth.
"Be not dismayed," said the father to the lamb,
"My salvation is forever and my righteousness stand still.

Fear not the reproach of men or their reveling,
I am the witness that you are the covenanted one.
I have refined and chosen you in the furnace of afflict
Continue to be faithful, and I will bring you justice.

What I have joined together must no man discord.
Be learned, my little ones—guard your choices of mate.
I admonish you wisely—Be not unequally yoked."

LOVE CONQUERS ALL

Have you ever been to the far Middle East?
Where there's no peace and love to feast,
Only fighting and hatred without cease,
Even the cradle's at war, if you please.

They rejected Christ who cannot compromise,
Their eyes are blinded, they cannot see the light.
Being in darkness, they cannot comprehend,
What a pity! If only they accepted the Messiah then.

But we understand that Jesus Christ came and died for us,
Without a doubt, we accepted His love.
Hence, we're a peculiar people, a chosen generation,
Not only the children of the light but hired watchmen.

According to the scriptures, their blood is in our hands,
If we do not sound the alarm of Love and Peace to stand.
Therefore we need to love in spite of despise,
Because we serve a God of love, not disguise.

Let's reconsider—it's only a test to see who's best,
Man is like the flower of the grass to contest.
For the earth is the Lord's, my friend,
Whose Love conquers all to amend.

Made in United States
Orlando, FL
11 December 2024

55461340R00055

Manufactured by Amazon.ca
Bolton, ON

13492073R00053